small
DREAMS

Jeffrey Milstein

50 PALM SPRINGS TRAILER HOMES

Schiffer Publishing Ltd®

4880 Lower Valley Road • Atglen, PA 19310

Cover & Interior Design by Danielle D. Farmer
On the cover: Palm Springs 19, Modern, Sahara Mobile Home Park
On the contents: close up of backlit palm tree fronds © Patjo. Courtesy of www.bigstockphoto.com.

Type set in Langdon / Mr Keningbeck / Futura Std

ISBN: 978-0-7643-5247-8
Printed in China

Published by Schiffer Publishing, Ltd.
4880 Lower Valley Road
Atglen, PA 19310
Phone: (610) 593-1777; Fax: (610) 593-2002
E-mail: Info@schifferbooks.com
Web: www.schifferbooks.com

For our complete selection of fine books on this and related subjects, please visit our website at www.schifferbooks.com. You may also write for a free catalog.

Schiffer Publishing's titles are available at special discounts for bulk purchases for sales promotions or premiums. Special editions, including personalized covers, corporate imprints, and excerpts, can be created in large quantities for special needs. For more information, contact the publisher.

We are always looking for people to write books on new and related subjects. If you have an idea for a book, please contact us at proposals@schifferbooks.com.

OTHER SCHIFFER BOOKS ON RELATED SUBJECTS:

Palm Springs: Mid-Century Modern,
Dolly Faibyshev, ISBN 978-0-7643-3461-0

Palm Springs Mid-Century Modern Postcard Book,
Dolly Faibyshev, ISBN 978-0-7643-4521-0

FOREWORD

In his latest photographic study, *small***DREAMS: 50 PALM SPRINGS TRAILER HOMES**, New York photographer Jeffrey Milstein has documented trailers or mobile homes in Palm Springs, California, and nearby Rancho Mirage. Milstein is a nationally recognized photographer whose previous studies include the award-winning *Aircraft*, which received first place in the PDN'S Pix Digital Imaging Contest (2005), *Cars of Cuba, LA Aerials, NY Aerials,* and many others. In this book, Milstein's subjects started life as prefabricated steel structures transported to their sites; his photographs reveal the human propensity to customize one's home. In some cases, the ribbed steel casing, aluminum framed windows, and other manufactured features are clearly visible. Others display every effort to disguise the origins of the unit. This exercise ranges from a partial re-skinning of the exterior with wood siding or the addition of a front porch or side carport, to virtually repackaging the trailer in contemporary architectural styles ranging from the California ranch house to desert modern, colonial revival, and Egyptian revival.

Individual landscape treatments are key to giving the trailers a unique identity. The configuration of the site necessarily played a role: most units are backed into their sites and have limited setback from the road; others are on corners and have two or more exposures. As recorded in Milstein's photos, some homeowners may choose to create miniaturized front lawns edged with a variety of concrete blocks and filled with plants and lawn. Other owners keep the maintenance to a minimum, using tinted concrete (often coordinated with details on the trailer) or gravel and iconic desert plants—cacti and palms are especially popular.

When photographing the trailers, Milstein imposes a consistent visual grid on his subjects: viewed from the front and symmetrically composed, with sufficient foreground to capture the relationship of the trailers and their setting to the road and the desert backdrop of palm trees, mountains, and blue skies. The position of the sun varies in the images, but in the editing process, Milstein objectifies surface reflections and shadow patterns in much the same way that photo realistic painters Richard Estes and Robert Bechtle did. The result is a distancing from the subject matter, turning the series into a scientific study of a species or type.

The photo historian Patricia McDonnell places Milstein's work in the photographic tradition of "typologizing, that is, creating a virtual registry of variation upon a theme to better grasp a clearly defined cultural meaning."[1] This puts his work into the fine company of August Sander and Hilla and Bernd Becher. Milstein's work was included in *New Typologies* in New York (2008), organized by noted photography curator Martin Parr. Their commentary on the built environment also echoes the photographic studies of Edward Ruscha and Lewis Baltz, as well as Robert Venturi and Denise Scott Brown's studies of Levittown.

The question of type has particular meaning in an architectural context. Early twentieth–century architectural theorists saw it as synonymous with notions of standardization. In this country, designers interested in finding ways to meet the housing demands of a growing population sought to exploit methods of mass production artfully developed by the automobile industry. At the same moment, trailers were invented as a product of the "back-to-nature" movement, making it possible for the motoring tourist to bring along the comforts of home while enjoying the outdoors.

The growth of the trailer industry reflected these dual associations in its products—as affordable housing that could serve the needs of seasonal as well as year-round housing. By the 1930s, carefully designed trailer parks were laid out to accommodate the units. In urban areas the parks were sited near major transportation routes on open or former agricultural land. In many communities these parks were seen as low-income enclaves. Sensitive to this association, the trailer industry renamed its products "mobile homes" in the early 1950s, but the dual nomenclature prevails today.[2]

Trailer parks in Palm Springs and other neighboring communities of the Coachella Valley did not suffer the same stigma as was found elsewhere in the country.[3] Palm Springs was, and still is, receptive to new settlement by a range of income groups, despite its image as an "ultrasmart winter resort for movie stars and with the Hollywood set and people who like and can afford to live where and as movie stars live."[4] Many of the trailer parks were built along or near State Route 111, which provided primary automotive access to the desert communities in the years prior to the construction of the interstate system. Milstein's images were shot in several trailer parks. They include Blue Skies in Rancho Mirage, developed by Bing Crosby with streets named for movie stars; the Sahara Mobile (originally Sahara Trailer) Home Park; and Horizon Trailer Village in Palm Springs.

Whatever one's income level, life in a trailer assumes the residents have adapted to living in a limited space. This condition varies depending on the specifics of the unit—but for Milstein, who as a young architect designed several prototypical small, economical kit houses, the trailer evoked a long-standing interest. Two of his small house concepts were published in *Family Circle*—his 192-square-foot "Bolt-Together House" (1972) and the 180-square-foot "Summer House" (1980). His "Tent House" (1975), a mere eighty-eight square feet, appeared in *Popular Science*. In each project, Milstein sought to create efficient spaces that could be built economically through the use of standard-dimensioned materials available to the public in home improvement stores.[5]

Milstein's book focuses on familiar objects of everyday life—the trailer or mobile home. He collects them photographically, as he has described other works, "like a book of botanicals or a *Peterson's Guide to Birds*," into a series of beautiful pictures, presenting them in a way you don't normally see them. The chaos of their larger settings is filtered out and one is left to examine the trailers' commonalities and distinguishing features added by their owners. Milstein, a California native, understands that the easy-going culture of the California desert is the ideal laboratory to examine the trailers as a typology of human habitation.

—**LAUREN WEISS BRICKER, PHD.**
associate professor of architecture,
California State Polytechnic University, Ponoma

1. Patricia McDonnell, "Aircraft: The Jet as Art by Jeffrey Milstein," for the Ulrich Museum of Art: Wichita State University, 2008.
2. Allan D. Wallis, Wheel Estates: *The Rise and Decline of Mobile Homes* (New York: Oxford University Press, 1991), 133.
3. Sian Winship, "Trailer Park/Mobile Home Community Development," for Historic Resources Group, *City of Palm Springs: Citywide Historic Context Statement*, 2015.
4. Federal Writers' Project of the Works Progress Administration, *California: A Guide to the Golden State* (New York: Hastings House, 1939), 628.
5. Lester Walker, *A Little House of My Own: 47 Grand Designs for 47 Tiny Houses* (New York: Black Dog & Leventhal Publishers), 1987.

ACKNOWLE

I would like to acknowledge and thank the following people for helping bring this book to light:

Bob Morton, my tireless editor, agent, and friend; Pete Schiffer of Schiffer Publishing; and Lauren Weiss Bricker for her thoughtful foreword;

My galleries that continue to support my work: **Kopeiken Gallery** in Los Angeles, **Benrubi Gallery** in New York, and **Bau-Xi Gallery** in Toronto;

Kim Cantine for always being there with encouragement and special late-night editing advice;

Jolie Andler Milstein for sharing her love of Palm Springs, **Val Andler** for sterling accommodations, and my daughter, **Lucy**, who keeps me young;

Helena Kaminski and **Anna Clem,** my studio assistants, who keep the wheels turning and have learned to deal with me changing my mind a lot;

Jeff Hirsch, my photographic personal shopper;

and all the people from the trailer parks featured who created the homes and allowed me to photograph them.

GMENTS

INTRODUCTION

Before I devoted myself full-time to photography, I trained and worked as an architect, and found that I was always attracted to economy of scale and owner-built indigenous architecture. So when I began photographing mid-twentieth-century architecture in Palm Springs, I was especially drawn to the unique trailer parks of the area. There I saw virtually identical basic modules—the long, narrow, box-like shape of the dwelling, flanked by a carport and a portico—made distinctive and personal by their owners in a wonderful variety of ways with the addition of decorative elements and landscaping. Seeing these homes reminded me that when I was about twelve years old I had gone to a Saturday matinee at the Del Mar movie theater in Los Angeles, and for fifteen cents watched the movie *The Long, Long Trailer,* starring Lucille Ball and Desi Arnaz. For me, a third star was the building of the title, a big yellow metal travel trailer. I was fascinated by it, and later learned that it was a 1953 thirty-six-foot Redman "New Moon" model, which sold for $5,345 at the time. And now, more than a half century later, I discovered that these were the types of trailers that formed the nucleus of many of the homes in the trailer parks I photographed. What was special about them, and made them so visually appealing, was that over the years they had been lovingly added to and decorated so that they became more than mere houses. They were highly personal, individualized homes reflecting each owner's dreams.

Palm Springs 01 / Original Trailer, Sahara Mobile Home Park

Palm Springs 02 / Sahara Mobile Home Park

Palm Springs 03 / Sahara Mobile Home Park

Palm Springs 04 / Sahara Mobile Home Park

Palm Springs 05 / Sahara Mobile Home Park

Rancho Mirage 06 / Blue Skies Village

Palm Springs 07 / Sahara Mobile Home Park

Palm Springs 08 / Sahara Mobile Home Park

Palm Springs 09 / Sahara Mobile Home Park

Palm Springs 10 / Sahara Mobile Home Park

Palm Springs 11 / Sahara Mobile Home Park

Palm Springs 12 / Sahara Mobile Home Park

Palm Springs 13 / Sahara Mobile Home Park

Palm Springs 14 / Sahara Mobile Home Park

Rancho Mirage 15 / Blue Skies Village

Rancho Mirage 16 / Blue Skies Village

Rancho Mirage 17 / Blue Skies Village

Rancho Mirage 18 / Blue Skies Village

Palm Springs 19 / Sahara Mobile Home Park

Palm Springs 20 / Sahara Mobile Home Park

Palm Springs 21 / Sahara Mobile Home Park

Rancho Mirage 22 / Blue Skies Village

Rancho Mirage 23 / Blue Skies Village

Rancho Mirage 24 / Blue Skies Village

Rancho Mirage 25 / Blue Skies Village

Rancho Mirage 26 / Rancho Mirage Mobile Home Park

Palm Springs 27 / Sahara Mobile Home Park

Palm Springs 28 / Sahara Mobile Home Park

Rancho Mirage 29 / Blue Skies Village

Palm Springs 30 / Sahara Mobile Home Park

Rancho Mirage 31 / Blue Skies Village

Palm Springs 32 / Sahara Mobile Home Park

Palm Springs 33 / Sahara Mobile Home Park

Palm Springs 34 / Sahara Mobile Home Park

Palm Springs 35 / Sahara Mobile Home Park

Palm Springs 36 / Sahara Mobile Home Park

Rancho Mirage 37 / Blue Skies Village

Palm Springs 38 / Sahara Mobile Home Park

Palm Springs 39 / Sahara Mobile Home Park

Palm Springs 40 / Sahara Mobile Home Park

Palm Springs 41 / Sahara Mobile Home Park

Palm Springs 42 / Sahara Mobile Home Park

Palm Springs 43 / Sahara Mobile Home Park

Palm Springs 44 / Sahara Mobile Home Park

Palm Springs 45 / Sahara Mobile Home Park

Palm Springs 46 / Sahara Mobile Home Park

Palm Springs 47 / Sahara Mobile Home Park

Rancho Mirage 48 / Blue Skies Village

Palm Springs 49 / Blue Skies Village

Palm Springs 50 / Sahara Mobile Home Park

Palm Springs 51 / Sahara Mobile Home Park

Palm Springs 52 / Sahara Mobile Home Park

Jeffrey
MILSTEIN

Jeffrey Milstein is a photographer, architect, graphic designer, and pilot. His photographs have been exhibited and collected throughout the United States and Europe, and are currently represented in the US by Paul Kopeikin Gallery in Los Angeles and Bonni Benrubi Gallery in New York City. In 2012, Milstein's work was presented in a solo show at the Smithsonian National Air and Space Museum. His photographs have been published in the *New York Times*, *Los Angeles Times*, *Harper's*, *Time*, *Fortune*, *American Photo*, *Eyemazing*, *Die Ziet*, *Wired*, *PDN*, *Esquire*, *BuzzFeed*, *Slate*, *Huffington Post*, and *Conde Nast Traveler*, and seen on the CBS Evening News with Scott Pelley. Born in Los Angeles, where he frequently returns to photograph, Milstein makes his home in Woodstock, New York. His website is www.jeffreymilstein.com.